ALS: THE GIFT OF A DESIGNER DISEASE

Personal reflections on living with a chronic disease, growing old, and just living

WILLIS J. MERRIMAN

Bill (Willis) Merriman

ISBN: 0615953603
ISBN-13: 9780615953601

DEDICATION

For Suzie and Tim, members of my first ALS support group led by Selma Searfoss. I was the "old man" in our group of three. Tim had teenage daughters and Suzie had a small child. Both had the greater part of their lives ahead of them. ALS claimed their lives before they had a chance to fully live them.

CONTENTS

ACKNOWLEDGMENTS

How does one acknowledge people and groups who have been a part of my journey with ALS for over two decades? "Acknowledgment" is really not an appropriate a word. A more appropriate word is a heartfelt "thanks." Thanks to the following groups and persons for making my journey tolerable, informative, humorous, and not without hope:

The ALS Association of Connecticut
Special thanks to Joan Patten Argento, Andy Braun Byrne, Anne Grosso Davino, and Jeannie Asper Walsh

The ALS Association Minnesota/North Dakota/South Dakota Chapter
Special thanks to Lisa Kronk

The Muscular Dystrophy Association (MDA) of Connecticut

The ALS Clinic in Connecticut held first at the University of Connecticut Medical Center and then at the Hospital for Special Care

Special thanks to the ALS Clinic members, especially to Dr. Randall Benson, the neurologist who first recognized that I had ALS; Dr. Kevin Felice, the neurologist who watched and guided my progress through my first eleven years with the disease; and nurse Candace Kiely

The ALS Clinic of Excellence at Hennepin County Medical Center, Minneapolis

Hannah Kraicer, who used a draft of this manuscript at Queens University, Kingston, Ontario, Canada

PREFACE

Many Americans became aware about amyotrophic lateral sclerosis (ALS), Lou Gehrig's disease, with the publication of the book *Tuesdays with Morrie*. Mitch Albom wrote it about Morrie Schwartz, his former college professor who was dying from the disease. The book was published in 1997. I was diagnosed with the disease two years earlier. The book by Albom told Morrie's story well and captured the attention of many people worldwide. Morrie's story, based on Albom's book, was made into a TV movie in 1999.

Like other readers, I deeply appreciated Albom's book. The only problem was that it is written in the third person standing outside the person suffering with the disease. I did not fully comprehend this until I discovered that in 1996, a year before Albom's book, Morrie Schwartz had written a book, *Morrie in His Own Words*, about his life with ALS.

While it may be not as well written as *Tuesdays with Morrie* or appeal to as large a readership as Albom's book, I felt a kinship with Morrie. It was written from within a person who was struggling with the same disease that I and many others struggled with.

At any given time, there are 30,000 people who have ALS in the United States. About 5,600 people are diagnosed with the disease each year. I am one of them. This is my story. It is about the struggles, the anxiety, the grief, the laughs, and, yes, the gift of ALS.

A word about the title: book titles either describe what the book is about or are created to entice a reader to read or buy the book. Although people with ALS share similar symptoms, they often have symptoms seldom seen in others. For example, the average person with ALS lives only three to five years. However, I have lived more than five times that span. (A word about life expectancy of people living with ALS: Primary sources on the subject often differ. You may notice the differences in this document. An average of my studies indicate that 50 percent of the people who have ALS live at least three years after being diagnosed; 20 percent live five or more years; 10 percent live ten or more years; and 5 percent live twenty years or longer.)

While attending a symposium on ALS, I heard a researcher describe the disease's symptoms. One I often have was not mentioned. I have hyper reflexes. When the phone rings or I hear an unexpected loud noise, my whole body jerks. If I am holding a cup of coffee in my hands, the coffee takes flight. When I sold my condo a few years back, I had to replace much of the carpeting before putting it on the market due to the coffee stains.

When asked, the researcher responded, "I did not cover your particular symptom because it is not common among most people who have ALS." Although ALS may affect people differently, I found that living with it for over two decades allows me to see the common similarities and the differences in "persons with ALS" (PALS).

While this book is primarily about ALS, it may be helpful to many others. Those who have any chronic disease, caregivers, those who belong to the gerontology set, or those of any age group may find it as a possible blueprint for living.

LIVING WITH YOUR GIFTS

> "Yesterday is history, tomorrow is a mystery, and today is a gift; that's why they call it the present."
> —Eleanor Roosevelt (1884–1962)

It has taken me over seven decades to live with and use the gifts my creator has given me. Perhaps I am just a slow learner. It took a tragedy to teach me lessons that many people learn earlier in life and that some people never learn. What brought this miraculous change?

It began twenty years ago. My neurologist, Dr. Kevin Felice, diagnosed my speech difficulties to be caused by amyotrophic lateral sclerosis (ALS), Lou Gehrig's disease. There is no known cause. There is no known cure. Upon being diagnosed with ALS, patients usually have a life expectancy of two to five years, according to textbooks and medical journals.

Most persons with ALS (PALS) do not have the luxury of learning that ALS may be a gift. Fortunately, I have. I beat the odds. I have lived two decades with ALS. There is a clinical reason for the extremely slow progress of the disease in me. Neurologists must detect ALS in both the upper and lower neurons of the patient. The upper motor neurons (cells) are in the brain. The lower motor neurons are in the spinal cord. For me the disease is more concentrated in the upper motor neuron area, which is why I was one of the 10 percent who have lived with ALS at least ten years. In fact, I am now fortunate to be among the 5 percent who have had the disease twenty or more years.

I experience the ups and downs of coping with ALS like all other PALS. At times I want to scream and give up. Each time I met with my support group I received the courage to live on.

Of my original support group, I am the only one still living. At the time I was fast becoming a septuagenarian. I had lived a rich, full life. The others had their lives before them. Some had yet to have the thrill of holding their first child. Others had children excited about passing their driver's test and anticipating high school graduation.

It took ten years of struggling with ALS to realize that perhaps it is a gift. A minister friend of mine noticed it almost from the beginning. He would say, and still does, "Bill, God is not through with you yet."

I am still getting use to the idea that ALS is a gift and the unusual circumstance that caused the idea to literally pop into my thinking.

I was a patron of Goodspeed Opera House Musicals in Connecticut. One night, my usual companion was not available to attend so I invited Selma Searfoss. Selma is a social worker and led the first MDA ALS support group I attended.

The musical was *Flight of the Lawn Chair Man*. It is based on a true story of a man kept from achieving his impossible dream by a domineering mother and being tied to a nowhere job. He wanted to fly. With the love of a woman who said that he could do anything he set out to do, his dream came true. With his love by his side, he attaches helium-filled balloons to a lawn chair and takes flight.

At dinner after the theater, Selma and I talked about our own lives and how true to life the musical was. Too often people do not achieve their deepest ambitions because they are held back either by their own thinking or lack of encouragement from family and friends.

In the course of our conversation, coming out of nowhere, I said, "I don't know why I am saying this, but I am beginning to look on ALS as a gift." This is my story of the peculiar and devastating gift called ALS.

THE SEARCH

At the age of sixty-two, I took up downhill skiing. A year later I was in Stowe, Vermont, taking to the slopes at sixty-three. After a day of exercising muscles, bones, and sinew that had not been used for three wonderful New England seasons, I decided to call my daughters in California. Both of them, to my surprise (and theirs), asked puzzled, "Dad, have you been drinking?" They noticed a slurring and hesitancy in my speech. I also noticed that it sounded exactly like I was inebriated. The next morning, my speech was back to normal.

During the next year, I noticed the same recurring speech pattern. It was not consistent nor all that frequent. Those who knew me best were more aware of my unusual speech pattern than were strangers. Once, while on a flight from Boston to London, I was talking to some vineyard owners from South Africa and in the middle of a sentence I paused and apologized for my speech. They hadn't noticed anything wrong.

Through the next year, in meetings, public events, and sometimes over the telephone, I was reluctant to speak. I would preface my remarks with "I apologize for my slurring and slowness of speech." I also noticed that when speaking passionately to an issue, my lower jaw became rigid, with more frequent occurrences. I decided it was time for a complete physical.

I had always been blessed with good health. I told my primary physician that I thought I might have had a slight stroke. My mother had had one a number of years ago, and it affected her speech, which soon returned to normal. After one of the most thorough physicals I ever had, my doctor said that I was in good health. For my speech difficulties, he referred me to a neurologist.

The neurologist said my reflexes were brisk and my tongue was "hyper." I am a clergy and have done a great deal of public speaking. I am sure my audiences would agree that I have a hyper tongue. My neurologist wasn't sure what was causing my speech difficulty. He scheduled me for a magnetic resonance imaging (MRI).

An MRI bombards you with magnetic and radio waves to take images of your head or of your whole body. In my case, it was my head. There were some people who said (or who have always said) I ought to have my head examined. Well! This was it.

I was given earplugs and told to remain perfectly still. My body was moved into a large cylinder and I was surrounded by magnets. I heard all kinds of weird noises, some grinding and some that sounded like jackhammers. After about a half hour, I was moved out of the cylinder and told that my doctor would receive a report.

The next time I visited my primary physician. He said that my MRI was normal and showed no sign of a stroke. I then asked him for a diagnosis of my speech impediment and what could be done. His response was "I don't know." My last words to him were "Well then, I'll just have to live with it." This was in late October 1997.

In January, I accepted a speaking engagement in Los Angeles. Again, I was reluctant to accept. I had not made a major speech since I became aware of my speech problem. As I delivered the speech, I was constantly aware of the difficulty I was having in speaking normally. Thank God for the brain's computer! When I realized that I was going to have difficulty pronouncing a particular word, my computer brain would kick in and find another word—easier to pronounce without it being too noticeable. After that experience, I was determined, more than ever, to get to the bottom of my problem.

When I returned to Connecticut, I scheduled an appointment with an internist at the Glastonbury Clinic. He was replacing my primary physician who was taking a health leave. I was impressed with the young doctor. He was as determined as I was to diagnose my problem. When he learned that I had not gone back to my neurologist, he immediately counseled me to schedule an appointment and to take my MRI images with me. He then told me to get back to him with the results.

My second visit to the neurologist, whom I shall call neurologist number one, was rather strange. When he greeted me, his first words were "Is this your first visit?" I then explained that I had been to see him before, and my file was soon found. I repeated my story and handed him my MRI images. He didn't look at them but relied on the MRI specialist's description and evaluation. He proceeded with the neurological examination.

I was tapped with a reflex hammer on my limbs and my face, walked on my toes and my heels, and said "Ah!," at least a dozen times, with a wooden depressor pressed on the flat part my of tongue and against its sides. He observed every muscle and reflex in my body. After my examination, we returned to his office to discuss what he had found.

He told me that my reflexes, including my tongue, were brisk and that my MRI was normal. This I already knew. He gave me the impression that there was nothing more he could do. I urged him to think of something. Finally, he looked at me rather hesitantly.

"There is another test, but you may not want to hear the results." I practically had to drag the words out of him. "The results may show that you may have amyotrophic lateral sclerosis (ALS), Lou Gehrig's disease." His words set off a clanging in my mind. The little I knew about ALS told me that it was fatal, and if it turned out that I had it, I would not achieve my goal of living a long life. I asked for the test. It was given two hours later.

The test was an electromyogram (EMG). An EMG can indicate muscle disorders. The test consists of inserting electrodes into the skin surface and into various muscles. Electric impulses are directed through the electrodes and the needle. The impulses from muscle reaction are recorded on an oscilloscope. The electromyographer (usually a doctor trained in the workings of an EMG) reads the wave forms and is able to tell whether a disorder exists. The test was not as unpleasant as I was led to believe.

The doctor could not give me a complete report of the results of the EMG. He would have to study it and report to neurologist number one. We talked a long time, and he said that there was some indication of muscle disorder.

In the intervening week, before I called the neurologist for a complete report, I researched in books and on the Internet all I could find on ALS. The news was not encouraging. By the time ALS is diagnosed, you are already into what I call "the ALS process."

ALS is a "rapidly" progressive, "fatal" neuromuscular disease that attacks motor neurons responsible for transmitting electrical impulses from the brain to the voluntary muscles. Once diagnosed, there is an average life expectancy of between two and five years.

There are exceptions. The most notable is Stephen Hawking, the brilliant theoretical physicist. Hawking was diagnosed at the age of twenty-one. He is now in his seventies. He is confined to a wheelchair, has lost the use of his limbs, has difficulty in swallowing, and cannot talk.

As in Hawking's case, ALS does not affect the mind, nor is it contagious. It does not affect the senses of taste, sight, smell and hearing. It is thought that there is no pain. The cause is unknown and there is no known cure. My research left me anxious about the future, but in no way was I despondent. I looked forward to the results of my EMG.

My talk with the neurologist led me further into the dark–the unknown. He said that the results of my EMG were "vague." The only thing he could recommend was that I go to a speech therapist. Once again I trekked off to my primary-care physician. I was determined not to give up until I knew the root cause of my speech difficulties.

I shared my frustration with Dr. Paul D'Andrea at the Glastonbury Clinic. (From now on I will reveal the names of those doctors and therapists involved in my search for answers. They were not only helpful in my pursuit but also exemplify what I think the calling of medicine is all about.) Dr. D'Andrea authorized further blood tests and said that he would send my records to the Neurology Department at the University of Connecticut Medical Center. After they had received my records, I was to schedule an appointment with one of the neurologists at the center.

While I was waiting at the counter to have blood drawn for testing, two technicians were trying to decipher Dr. D'Andrea's handwriting to see what tests should be done. They confirmed with the doctor's office that it would be a blood test for bulbar palsy.* That was a new term for me. The blood was drawn and I went home to my own research on bulbar palsy.

My layperson's research told me that bulbar palsy might be related to my medulla oblongata, a part of the

---

* I have since learned, from Dr. Kevin Felice, that there is no test for bulbar palsy. He suggested it might have been a blood test for myasthenia gravis, which can produce hesitant speech. Whatever the test was, I was confronted with the term "bulbar palsy" and based my research on that issue. This underscores the difficulty in exploring all possible avenues before a diagnosis of ALS is made.

brain stem that controls speech and tongue movement. I further found out that the conditions and prognosis of bulbar palsy were no better than those for ALS.

Let me pause here and say something about a person's research into a field in which he or she knows little or almost nothing. The old adage is true: "A little knowledge is a dangerous thing." But when it comes to an individual's personal health, it is also too important to leave only to the experts. I was finding that my own personal research was like doing a picture puzzle. I was fast putting the straight-edged pieces together to form the border. The hard part was filling in the middle to get the complete picture. Personal research is important. But even more important is a healthy dialogue and the intelligent questions you should ask your physician.

Dr. D'Andrea called me a week later. My blood tests were normal. With this news and the fact that my appointment with the neurologist at the University of Connecticut Medical Center (UConn) was not for another two weeks, I took off on a trip to explore the Florida Everglades.

THE UNIVERSITY OF CONNECTICUT MEDICAL CENTER

I have visited many hospitals, and I have come in contact with numerous physicians because of my profession. But I was totally unprepared for what I found at the UConn Medical Center. My only contact with the facility prior to my March 31, 1998, appointment was the parking lot. I was there to pick up a rabbi friend and his wife from Pennsylvania.

They were having difficulty conceiving a child. They were told that for their particular problem there was only one doctor who could help them and she was at the UConn Medical Center. That was years ago, and they now have two children, naturally conceived.

People of Connecticut should become acquainted with the center. It is an architectural gem. The staff I met, physicians, therapists, nurses, technicians, and service people, were polite, courteous, and concern without being overbearing or "syrupy sweet." They were professionals, in the best sense of the word.

I am usually not enamored by hospital food, but I looked forward to eating in the food court at the center. Citizens of Connecticut should take pride in having such a facility.

My neurologist at the center was Dr. Randall Benson. I liked him immediately. Even though he had read my medical records, he wanted to hear about my problem in my own words. He then gave me a neurological examination. Although I had been through two of them before, I had the feeling that this examination was thorough and professional and would provide some answers. When Dr. Benson was finished, we discussed the findings at his desk. I recall it vividly.

His desk faced a wall. I was sitting at the side of the desk, with my back against the same wall, facing Dr. Benson. He was reviewing his notes, and I was asking questions. At one point I had my elbow on the desk, and he said, "Hold your hand just the way it is." He looked at the area between my thumb and first finger for what seemed to be a long time. He reflected and said, "You have a motor neuron disease. Its progress is very slow. However, in order to be sure, I have to rule out any other possibilities. I want to schedule another MRI and inject you with a fluid that will give better contrast." He did not specifically mention ALS. I knew, however, that ALS was a motor neuron disease.

Mentally, I was counting up how many years I had to live. As if reading my mind, Dr. Benson said that since it was progressing very slowly, I had many years ahead of me. He placed no limitations on me and suggested that I continue to live a normal life.

After our session, I went to the reception desk to set up appointments for an MRI and an examination by a speech therapist. While there, Dr. Benson sought me out and told me that Dr. Kevin Felice was conducting a clinical research trial on a new drug for ALS and that I might want to become a part of the study. There was that dreaded acronym again. Not since neurologist number one had I *really* heard the term or thought I that might have the disease. Dr. Benson had not used the term until that very moment in the reception area. Prior to that time he had used the amorphous term "motor neuron disease."

There is that "a little knowledge" adage again. My doctors and I were on a road to discovery. When Dr. Benson said that I had motor neuron disease, I had conveniently blocked out ALS in my mind. I do not think it was denial but just the fact that I did not know all the aspects of amyotrophic lateral sclerosis (ALS), Lou Gehrig's disease.

As I drove back to my home in Manchester, I thought, "I have ALS." For some reason I did not experience denial, nor anger, nor the "why-me syndrome." Don't read me wrong. I do not accept things blindly. My emotions run deep. But for some reason, I accepted the fact that I had ALS and would live with it to the best of my ability. This did not mean that I would not fight.

At home, all my emotions came to the surface. I phoned my youngest daughter in California. Lynette, who was director of admissions and student affairs for the nursing school at the University of Southern California (USC), had been following my medical journey with me. She aided me in my research and asked a friend—a pharmacy school professor—if he would help identify the best neurologists in the Northeast. It was the most difficult call I ever made.

My telephone bill also shows that it was one of the longest long-distance calls I ever made. I would have saved a lot of money if it had not been for the sobbing and for the long pauses in conversation to regain my composure. I finally got out the whole story. It was a good catharsis for both of us. We were both determined to not let my diagnosis get us down and to not live without hope.

Although my oldest daughter, Debra, was aware of my medical adventures, I had not mentioned the term "ALS" to her. She was going through a change of jobs at the time, and I did not want to add to her problems. I decided to tell her after I was approved for the drug research program. I later found out that my protection of her was unfounded.

I began a flurry of activities. I called Candace Kiely, RN, coordinator of the Sanofi Drug Study, to start the process to be included in the research program. Timing was crucial. The cutoff for inclusion was only six weeks away. A date was set for my first clinic visit, which was a screening process. I told her that my symptoms were almost entirely centered in my speech and not my muscles and reflexes. Fortunately, they were short of people whose ALS began in the bulbar region. Ms. Kiely would send the drug-testing protocol and a consent form to me.

At home, I began what I should have done years ago. Like many healthy adults, my thoughts were that it can always be done tomorrow. With the help of my Family Lawyer software, I drafted a living will, a regular will, and on the advice of an attorney, a durable power of attorney.

One day, I left my car over night at a garage for repairs. The next morning I decided to walk the two miles to the garage. I set off at a fast pace from my home when I suddenly stopped. I thought, "How much longer will I be able to take such walks?" In our fast-paced world I, like many others, lived the words from Richard Adler and Jerry Boss's musical, *The Pajama Game*: "We are racing with the clock. Hurry up! Can't waste time!" We drive at fast speeds on interstate highways and never look at the scenery. We never slow our pace to see the beauty and the needs of humanity.

When I resumed walking, I savored each step, taking in, for the first time, my neighborhood. I even stopped to smell the flowers.

THE SANOFI RESEARCH STUDY

Only one drug has been approved by the Food and Drug Administration for ALS. It is the drug Rilutek (riluzole). Clinical trials were done in the United States and Europe, and the drug adds about three months to a patient's life. Even so, the cost is prohibitive for many. The cost is between $800 and $1,000 per month. The Sanofi drug was being researched and tested at the University of Connecticut Medical Center and in over thirty research centers worldwide.

I read the drug protocol carefully and faxed it to my daughter at USC. She, in turn, shared it with some of her colleagues who were familiar with drug-testing research. Their opinions were faxed to me. As a result, I had many questions to answer myself and for the research team.

My first clinic visit was a screening session that lasted about five hours. I was given a complete physical examination. This included an electrocardiogram (ECG) and a spirometer test, which measures lung function and capacity. Blood was drawn for a detailed analysis as well as DNA for the 2D6 gene. A small number of ALS cases, called Familial ALS, suggest the significance of a hereditary factor.

I felt good about the tests. All my physical tests were within normal limits. After the testing, Candace went over the protocol, and I signed the consent form. She then went over a checklist concerning my breathing, swallowing, speaking, and physical dexterity. Except for my speech and occasional difficulty in swallowing, I was able to answer no to all the items on the checklist. Dr. Felice would conduct the last test of the day, discuss the study, and answer any questions that I might have.

Dr. Kevin J. Felice, a neurologist, the principal investigator for the project at UConn, once again gave me a complete neurological examination. Dr. Felice impressed me with his thoroughness. There was never any doubt in my mind that he was a man dedicated to his profession. In addition, he was the kind of person that you would like to have as a friend as well as your doctor.

In my research, I found that there are many diseases that have some of the same symptoms as ALS.

Documents directed me to seek out an ALS "expert," someone who sees many ALS patients. Dr. Felice was not only the principal investigator for the Sanofi study, he was in charge of the ALS Clinic at UConn and saw over two hundred ALS patients regularly each year.

After the examination, Dr. Felice and I had a long talk about ALS, and he very was thorough in answering my questions. He confirmed Dr. Benson's diagnosis that I had a motor neuron disease, and he wanted me in the study. He said that my "central nervous system" was affected by the disease but that my "peripheral nervous system" needed further examination. Parenthetically, "peripheral" is one of those words that is now difficult for me to pronounce. Before I could be admitted to the research program, I needed another EMG to further test my peripheral nerves. An appointment was set for the following week.

During the interim, I had my second MRI and a session with the speech therapist. I will discuss my speech therapy later but first want to say a word about my MRI and EMG at the UConn Medical Center. Their equipment is state of the art. I liken it to flying in a prop plane compared to the latest jets. The MRI was much quieter, and I was provided with headphones so I could listen to my choice of music.

The next week, my EMG was completely computerized with two colored monitors. Dr. Felice programmed the computer to receive the information that he sought. This time, I was measured on both my arms and legs for the exact placement of the electrodes. The needle electrode, for the first time, was inserted in parts of my face and my tongue. I can honestly say that I did not feel a thing. After the doctor and his assistant finished, I was told that I would learn of the results the next day.

The next day, Dr. Felice began with the words, "I really want you in the study." He then went on to say that the parameters of the Sanofi research did not allow him to say that I have Lou Gehrig's disease. Therefore, he could not admit me to the program. He explained why.

My central nervous system (the brain and spinal cord), consisting of betz cells, showed clear signs of the disease. My peripheral nervous system (the nerves that fan out to muscles, skin, internal organs, and glands), consisting of anterior horn cells, did not paint so clear a picture. ALS must show diffuse involvement of two or three limbs and the bulbar. The central nervous system involves a clinical diagnosis. The peripheral nervous system involves a clinical diagnosis and an EMG. My EMG was not definitive. That is why neurologist number one said the results of my first EMG were "vague." This does not mean that I did not have ALS. It does mean that its progress is slow and has not developed to the point where I could be included in the Sanofi research.

I was disappointed that I would not be able to participate in the study. I was encouraged by the slow progress of the disease. At one point I asked Dr. Felice if I should sell my three-story condo for a one-floor dwelling. He responded, "Not for a long time!" We then got into a philosophical discussion.

I had given a lot of thought about my quality of life and how I would cope with the progression of ALS. A life totally dependent upon others, without speech or the ability to feed myself, had been ruled out in my book.

Dr. Felice said that in Eastern cultures, quality of life is dependent more on the use of the mind rather than physical attributes. It is true that Stephen Hawking made his greatest contributions after he was diagnosed with ALS. Even now his brilliant mind is making contributions that far surpass the overwhelming majority of people in the world. I was not convinced that the road Stephen Hawking took was for me, but the seeds were planted.

Dr. Felice said he would send his findings to Dr. Benson. He personally wanted to follow my progress and said he would see me about every three months.

Driving home, I thought about how fortunate I was, even though I had not passed the screening for the drug study. I had had every test imaginable for ALS and was examined by one of the leading ALS neurologists in Connecticut. I had a lot to be thankful for.

SPEECH THERAPY

I had five sessions with a speech therapist. My first two were with Mr. Carl Coehlo, who normally teaches at the University of Connecticut, Storrs. Carl takes time off from his teaching periodically to keep his "hands-on" experience current. He shared my own prejudice that most professionals need what I call "a reality break."

Carl gave me lessons in "Breathing and Swallowing 101," as well as a lesson in the anatomy that goes with it. As I noted previously, I had difficulty at times swallowing. This would happen, not too frequently, while eating. When it did, it felt as though my food went down the wrong passageway. When this happens, I can only speak in low rasping whispers for about five minutes until my voice gets back to normal. He told me that my mother was correct. Never try to eat and talk at the same time. Since Carl's advice, in a two-month interval, the problem had not reoccurred. Carl also showed me some rudiments of my speech pathology and how to deal with my speech difficulties.

My second therapist, Ms. Lisa Pavia, was extremely helpful. One truth she shared set me on the right track. Early in our first session, she said she would give me the tools to manage my speech problems. I thought that one day I would wake up in the morning and my speech would be back to normal. When I did regular radio and television shows in my professional life, I consciously developed slower and more deliberate speech, always speaking from my diaphragm. I had become lazy and was speaking, for the most part, from my throat up. Lisa advised me to rediscover those lost skills and use them in normal speaking.

Lisa gave me exercises in breathing and various notes and sounds to practice. I did them faithfully every day. The only drawback, honestly, was that the person in the next townhouse had put her condo up for sale. Now that it was summer and the windows were open, we might have a mass exodus.

It was obvious that Lisa worked with a number of ALS patients. She anticipated future difficulties and showed me swallowing techniques and how changing syllabic emphasis on different words would help me manage more effectively.

I would rate my five sessions of speech therapy very high. They gave the right tools to correct some bad habits and develop correct new ones. I was taught how to cope and above all given a sense of humor about my difficulties.

I had another session with Dr. Benson. He had all the results of the many tests that were given, and he even passed some of them on to Dr. D'Andrea. He assured me that the progress was slow and advised me to add some new countries to my many travels. He then put into words something that I was slowly finding out. He said that we diagnose ALS through elimination of all other possibilities. He then said, "With motor neuron disease doctor and patient work as a team. We learn from each other."

I was signed up for my first session with the ALS Clinic at UConn. There were only thirteen ALS Clinics at that time in the United States. It is a process where the progress of people with ALS is followed by a medical team of doctors, specialists, and therapists. I looked forward to it.

I lived a normal life. I continued to write, ride my bike, and work out three times each week at a health center. Eighteen years later, that is now in the dim past.

I CAN'T GET A WORD IN EDGEWISE

The best compliment I ever received about my speaking ability was by a former governor of Wisconsin. It was in 1970, and at the time he was president of the University of Wisconsin at Stevens Point. Lee Dreyfus was an excellent communicator and a popular professor of speech. I was aware of his presence when I got up to speak at a gathering in Madison, Wisconsin. He preceded me with an excellent address, and I was hesitant to follow. When I was finished speaking on the subject of "Writing Your Own Obituary," Dreyfus approached me and said, "I am glad I didn't follow you."

I always had the gift of being a good speaker. My mother would say that I had the gift of gab. Speech is a powerful tool, and speakers have to be aware of its power for both good and bad. Hopefully, I used my speech wisely. It was my intention to arouse a spirit of social justice and peace and to open the windows to all that is beautiful and lovely through regular speaking engagements and on radio and television.

Recently, Harpo has become my favorite Marx brother. He was the one with the curly red wig who did not speak. He communicated through a brass horn with an attached black rubber ball. A squeeze of the ball by the comedic Harpo not only produced a honk from the horn, but belly laughs from Harpo's audience. In real life, Harpo was very talkative and a good conversationalist. On stage, he was a zany mime always good for a laugh. He writes of his antics in his autobiography *Harpo Speaks!* and that his son Bill wanted Harpo to call the book *What's the Use Talking?*

I have identified with Harpo's stage presence ever since my speech therapist told me that there might be a time when I cannot speak. Since my professional life was dependent, in a large part, on my speaking ability, I was particularly alarmed when the onset of Lou Gehrig's disease (ALS) began with my speech. My speech has become slurred, halting, and slower. People who know me aren't as bothered by it as I am. For many years after my diagnosis, people who had never heard me talk thought my speech was normal but slow. My change in speech is very aggravating to me personally. There are times when I want to buy a curly red wig and a honking horn. By imitating Harpo I would at least get a laugh.

I had never met a person with ALS before my diagnosis. In the years I have had ALS, I have met many people with motor neuron diseases, including ALS. They come in all shapes, sizes, and ages. They are a wonderful lot and come from many walks of life. Motor neuron disease is a great leveler. There is never the question, even in the back of our minds, of social or economic status or of one's job or profession. We are all equal. We have common enemy, and we are determined to fight it.

The frustrating part about my speech is that everybody wants to get in the last word, and I can't get a word in edgewise. They are always finishing my sentences or filling in the last word. Once in a while someone says, "Eh?" or "What's that you said?" Either everybody is suddenly losing their hearing or I am messing up my words. It is especially difficult when talking on the phone.

I remember learning in graduate school that Moses was slow of speech and that Noah had difficulty talking. Some commentators said that Senator Ted Kennedy stuttered. Of course the prime example is Stephen Hawking, who has ALS. He cannot speak or take care of his daily needs. This has not stopped him from sharing his vast knowledge with the world.

A rather amusing but tragic incident happened when my daughter, Debra, and I were driving from Los Angeles to San Francisco. It was late at night, and I was pulled over by the highway patrol for a traffic violation. Hearing my slurred speech, the officer thought I was intoxicated and wanted to give me a Breathalyzer test. Frustrated, I yelled out, "I am not drunk! I have Lou Gehrig's disease and that is why I talk this way." He immediately backed off as though I had leprosy. Needless to say, I didn't get a ticket.

Since my speech has changed, I try various ways to compensate. I avoid multi-syllable words and often plan ahead on what I am going to say. Many times with strangers, I apologize for my speech, and they are usually polite by saying they didn't notice. My speech pathologist showed me how to pronounce words that begin with vowels. I now pronounce a long vowel instead of shortening it.

Another disadvantage of my diminishing speech capacity is that I can no longer sing. My daughters would say that this is nothing new. But I love to sing even though I probably cannot carry a tune. I now sing in my mind. Therein is one of the advantages. I can sound like Sinatra or one of the three tenors. It is too bad that the world will never know.

In meetings I spend a lot more time listening than talking, and I have made some amazing discoveries. People do not listen. They like to hear themselves talk. They are planning what they are going to say next. Have you ever noticed that the "talking heads" on television are always talking past each other? It is amazing that we ever accomplish anything. We no longer communicate or educate. We only talk.

I still get mad as hell about my loss or change in speech. I long to stand before an audience and practice my God-given art of persuasion and education. I want to hear people laugh and cry at my words. I want to see men and women, boys and girls get up after I have spoken and go out and change the world. But, alas, that part of my life is gone. I have to find other venues. I really believe that it is the creator's way of showing me another way.

My creative gifts are still intact. I have always written, but I now spend more time at it. Maybe the great American novel is hidden in the crevices of my mind. If not, that is not going to stop me from expressing myself or putting words on paper.

One of my friends was Suzie, who also had ALS. Suzie was in my first support group. She lost her capacity to speak, and she wrote everything on a slate that she carried with her. I learned a lot from my friend. We communicated without talking. Not being able to talk did not take the sparkle from her eyes.

I can no longer get a word in edgewise. Harpo was right. What's the use talking? Brooks, mountains, and trees cannot talk, but they speak volumes. My friend Suzie and I continued to do the same until she succumbed to ALS in her late twenties.

THE GIFT OF HUMOR

There is a thin line between comedy and tragedy. The tragedy of ALS is that there is no known cure. Most patients die within five years. Eight to 20 percent survive for at least ten years. Stephen Hawking, the renowned mathematician and physicist, has lived with ALS for fifty years.

People with any debilitating disease and their caregivers learn quickly how to cope. Psychological, physical, and mechanical devices are brought into play so that patients may continue to live a "normal" life. One key device, often overlooked, is laughter. If we focus on the tragedy of our illness we become remorse and depressed. It has a negative effect and runs counter to the inner self.

I have already mentioned my slurred speech, which confuses people about my level of intoxication. My ALS Clinic visits at the UConn Medical Center were always filled with mixed emotions. It was at these sessions that I learned how far my ALS had progressed and my prognosis. At one morning session, I needlessly apologized to my neurologist, Dr. Felice, about my slurred speech. He responded, "That's okay, Bill. I know that you like to take a nip or two before you come in."

That bit of humor instantly dissolved any anxieties that I had. It may have been a fleeting moment, but it was a key ingredient in dealing with any tragedy of life. It helps us to focus on life rather than death.

"While tragedy moves from sanity toward madness, comedy moves from madness toward sanity. In his pride, the tragic hero overreaches human limits and dies. In his folly, the comic hero ludicrously pounds his head against those limits, is brought to his senses, and lives" (*Time* magazine, January 2, 1965, theater section). A person who is facing any tragedy needs to pound his or her head against the limits and laugh. Life is for living, not dying. What better way to live than with a sense of humor.

Here are some illustrations from my own experience with ALS of honing my humor so I can laugh in the face of this deadly disease.

HUMOR AND HYPER-REFLEXES

Some PALS (people with ALS) may have hyper reflexes. My doctors say I have a hyper-tongue. I don't notice it myself, but my tongue is constantly wagging. I have never been much of a neighborhood gossip, so why is my tongue wagging? What I do notice is that I jump or have hyper reactions whenever the phone rings or I hear a loud noise.

One day the phone rang when I had a mug of coffee in my hand. My hand jerked and coffee spilled all over the rug. My reaction was frustration and a loud "DAMN!" It has happened many times. I have taken certain precautions for it to not happen. Occasionally, when it does, I look at the coffee on the rug and laugh. My tragedy turns to comedy, much like throwing a cream pie at a person in a black-and-white flick.

One day I was carrying a bag of groceries to my car. An attractive woman getting out of her car used her remote to lock the car, and it made the usual "beep" sound. My hands jerked, and my groceries went all over the parking lot. The woman who helped me pick up my groceries could not understand why I was laughing. I said it happens at home all the time. Aside from laughing at my plight, I made a new friend that day. It certainly beats taking out a personal ad.

I mentioned precautions to compensate for hyper reflexes. In the case of having a cup of hot coffee, I turn off the phone and put on my answering machine. An added benefit to this approach is that I have eliminated almost all telemarketing calls. When I was still able to go grocery shopping, I wheeled my groceries in the cart, no matter how few. This is no Einsteinium theory, but it worked for me.

Hyper-reflexes also affected my late cat and companion, Peaches. If I remember my Psychology 101 correctly, there was a Dutch psychologist who trained geese to imprint or imitate the psychologist's movements. Peaches imprinted my ALS-related hyper reflexes. When the phone rang or a loud noise was heard, Peaches jumped. This provided another form of comic relief.

Until her passing, Peaches was always underfoot. Because my footing is unsure, my legs give way and I fall easily. When I would walk in my house, she acted as a traffic cop walking in front of me, often back and forth diagonally. Occasionally she would stop and groom herself with no indication that she was causing me problems.

I used to try to prod her along with my cane, but she would never budge. Realizing she was not going to change, it was up to me to change. Rather than being frustrated, I pretended that she had gotten into my wine rack and just a bit tipsy. I enjoyed her antics.

I still can walk, but I spend most of my time in a motorized wheelchair or my lift chair. Up until her recent passing, Peaches again acted as a traffic cop. She would walk in front of my chair. When I stopped, even for a moment, she would stop and look both ways as if checking for traffic to clear. When I would start again, Peaches would proceed to lead the way with caution.

LIFE-CHANGING TRANSITION

A day I was dreading had arrived. I had to move from my three-story condo. I could still walk but not without a walker. Placing a walker on each floor and in the basement helped. Holding onto the railing as I climbed the stairs was not too difficult. I was even able to lift a walker into my Prius and go do my shopping.

I could provide for all my needs and received no outside help except a housekeeper who came every other week. My major problem was falling. Fortunately, the way I fell prevented major injuries. I fell like a rag doll. I seemed to become a Raggedy Ann or Andy doll and fall loosely and gently to the floor. I did not have to press the med-alert button around my neck once when I lived in Connecticut.

With the persuasion of my daughters and friends I decided to move. I needed a one-floor home that would be less draining of my limited physical resources. Since I had spent most of my life in the Midwest and had friends there who encouraged me, I looked for a one-floor home in Minneapolis, Minnesota.

My ALS clinic team in Connecticut, led by Dr. Kevin Felice, said that Minnesota had a number of excellent ALS clinics and that I would be well cared for.

With my condo sold and the purchase of a one-story home, I moved to the Land of Ten Thousand Lakes.

MOVING AND MAJOR CHANGES

When I moved back to Minnesota in 2008 I used a walker. Now I am nearly 24/7 in a sitting position either in my power wheelchair or in my lift chair. It is almost impossible to get to a standing position without a boost from my lift chair.

Before I had a power wheelchair I used to fall as many as three or four times a day. Since I live alone I would have to press the button tied around my neck and seek help through med-alert. I have pressed the med-alert button only a few times since using the power chair. Each time Minneapolis sent three of their finest from the fire department. In a matter of minutes they had me standing, which was all I needed.

Other times when I fell I found a unique way of getting to a standing position. I first check for any broken bones. Finding none I would scoot across the floor and sit on the top step leading to the basement. Then I would plant my feet on two steps below. Holding onto the railing, I would lift myself to a standing position. Usually my walker was nearby and I was ready to resume whatever I had to do before I fell.

A CHANGE IN ALS CLINICS AND MEDICAL ASSOCIATIONS

While living in Connecticut, all my medical and ALS needs were well met by doctors and therapists. I work closely with the state ALS Association and Muscular Dystrophy Association (MDA). MDA has an active ALS program and funds ALS research. I served for a time on the ALS Association board and watched it grow from an organization with no staff to a full-fledged and very competent staff.

The ALS Association and clinic staff became a part of me, a sort of extended family. I thought the change would be difficult. In reality, the change was seamless.

Dr. Felice in Connecticut recommended the ALS Clinic at Hennepin County Medical Center. This was confirmed by a friend who taught at the University of Minnesota Medical School and was a medical ethicist.

It was further confirmed by Candace Kylie, the ALS nurse at the clinic in Connecticut.

Candace had met Lisa Kronk, the patient service coordinator of the ALS Association of Minnesota and the Dakotas. On one of visits to Minnesota, I met with Lisa and the ALS Association staff. They convinced me that I was making the right choice.

One other factor was the high standards the National ALS Association sets for its clinics. While procedures may vary with each clinic, the quality of care is always excellent.

A word must be said about my first visit to the ALS Clinic at the Hennepin County Medical Center. After the usual weighing in and blood pressure and temperature being taken, I waited for first examiner to come in. I waited. I waited. I waited...

Finally, Dr. Scott Bundlie, neurologist, walked into the room. He was followed by six other neurologists who were learning about ALS. Dr. Bundlie apologized for his lateness. He and the other six neurologists were reading my sixty-page ALS medical report that Dr. Felice, my neurologist in Connecticut, had compiled.

My lasting memory of that first visit to the ALS clinic was being prodded and having the strength of my arms and legs tested by not one but seven neurologists.

One final word about ALS clinics: I received from my clinic a listing of all those who serve ALS patients and their expertise along with their pictures. I immediately wrote across the top of the page, in capital letters, "THE DREAM TEAM." As I posted it on my study wall, I thought that all ALS clinics are dream teams. They teach us how to cope, make our lives easier, and give us hope to live with this dreaded disease.

IT IS ALL ABOUT ATTITUDE: THE GIFT FROM BOB ZIMMERMAN, THE RAMP MAN

When I moved to Minnesota I graduated from walker to a wheelchair. I was in need of a ramp so I could be wheeled outdoors. The state of Minnesota provides a service for designing ramps. The design person is Bob Zimmerman.

I was ill prepared when Bob arrived at my home one morning. Bob is a large person with a wonderful sense of humor to match. He was always ready to tell a joke. In addition to designing ramps and having a good sense of humor, Bob had sound advice for people who are handicapped either by illness or just growing old.

On our initial visit, I said, "I am not going to let ALS get the best of me." Bob responded, "I hope you don't do what some people with disabilities do. They often ignore various aids that could make life easier for them. By not using these aids they lose what little strength they have and tire out."

Bob's advice struck close to home. Although I am now surrounded by such aids, I was slow in getting them. Perhaps I was just being stubborn. Saying "I am not going to let ALS get the best of me" was a way of gritting my teeth and doing things the way I always did even if it killed me.

Bob taught me that it is all about attitude. Chronic illness or the aging process is difficult. Having a positive attitude eases that process. This is especially true with aids to help.

THE GIFT OF BEING A KID AGAIN

> "To be a child and have no worries on my mind... To be a child again and have a child's faith in...Well I'm a man now and the world weights heavy on my shoulders and problems get bigger every day as I grow older...To be a child again...To be a child again"
> —Johnny Tillotson, songwriter and singer

How often do we as adults say these words when we see children playing or just having a good time? There may come a time when due to chronic illness or aging when we have to revert to our inner child. Rather than fight it, we should enjoy it. I should have realized that I would have the thrill of being a child again soon after I was diagnosed with ALS. In addition to the work of the ALS Association, the Muscular Dystrophy Association

(MDA) funds ALS research. When I was diagnosed with ALS I had become one of Jerry's *Kids*. This was strongly emphasized when I received my first monthly publication, *Quest*, from MDA. It was addressed "To the parents of Willis J. Merriman."

I once attended a meeting chaired by a woman in her fifties. She introduced her mother, who was in her eighties. Each member of the group then introduced themselves. When it was the chairwoman's mother's turn, she said, "My daughter has it wrong. I am the daughter. She is now my mother."

The mother, now a daughter, did not go into the particulars, but I know now what she meant. Each day there is a new revelation of how I am a kid again.

It should not be difficult to be a kid again. Adults have already returned to the picture books they enjoyed as a child. They now have apps (pictures) in place of cursive.

WHEELCHAIR/STROLLER: Minneapolis has many lakes. I used to enjoy walking or biking around them. Now I enjoy being pushed around in my wheelchair by a daughter or friend. Whenever I see a child being pushed around the lake in a stroller we usually smile or wink at each other knowing that this isn't so bad. It beats walking.

People who design wheelchairs should consult with a stroller design team. Strollers are much more comfortable and more pleasing to the eye. Why do wheelchairs always have to be basic black? They could use some color or maybe a floral design. I envy the children in strollers who wink at me as we pass each other. The colors and designs of their strollers celebrate life while I ride around in basic funeral black.

Before I mention the next item that reminds us of our childhood, I will return to my adult state for a moment. My speech therapist, confirmed by my nurse, said that many adults prefer more sophisticated (adult) terms than to use more common terms or language from their childhood. So...the next section will deal with the subjects of shirt guards, labial (lip) leakage, secretion management, excess secretions, and food spillage.

In kid language I will discuss bibs, drooling, and messy eating.

ADULT BIBS: There are younger men with gravy stains on their ties. Many adults spill food on their clothing. For some reason we adults think it more genteel, perhaps more sophisticated, for adults to have an occasional spill on their clothing rather than wear bibs. That's nonsense!

We adults have no hesitation wearing bibs when we eat lobster or spaghetti. Taking our cues from the highchair set, we should start a campaign for all adults to wear bibs. It would certainly save on our cleaning bills.

A whole new industry could be created, "Designer Bibs for Adults." Adults could buy bibs for different occasions. We could have bibs that we use only at home. Bibs for our favorite posh restaurant would be more formal compared to those we use at our favorite hamburger joint.

Remember Bob Zimmerman? He said it was all about attitude. When I finally decided to buy an adult bib, I did a Google search for "Adult Bibs." There were numerous websites for me to explore.

After looking at throwaway bibs and cloth bibs made of terry cloth or fine linen that could be washed, I found a company that must have heard Bob Zimmerman. It was a company that makes "Bibitudes." The company markets them as "Adult Bibs with Attitude."

I ordered two, one for everyday use and one to be used at formal dinners. As a person who frequently thinks and acts outside the box, my everyday bib reflects my personality. In the center of the bib is an empty plate surrounded by various foods. The caption is appropriate: "Think outside the plate." My second bib is much too formal to wear at home. There is a picture of a tuxedo jacket complete with boutonniere.

I wore my bibs only at home at first. Finally, on the day of an ALS clinic appointment, I took my bib with me. I had half decided to wear it to lunch after clinic.

At the session with my speech therapist and nutritionist, I mentioned bibs with attitude. Mary Ann, my nurse, pulled it out of the bag she always has with her.

She also puts my wallet and glasses in the bag because I have difficulty getting things out of my pocket.

My speech therapist responded to my Bibitude first. She said she wish she had known about bibs with attitudes for her mother. The nutritionist, who was a substitute, was enthralled with idea of my not being averse to calling a bib a bib. Due to their reaction, I used my Bibitude at a public restaurant. I wore it in a second restaurant. Both times there was positive and enthusiastic response. It inspired me to purchase two more bibs.

Whether you buy disposable "shirt guards" at your local convenience store or send away for them via the Internet, they are still bibs. There is nothing wrong with identifying with the toddler set. Our whole future is ahead of us.

MY BIBS (Bibs with attitude) used by permission of bibitudes.com

FINGERS, CHOPSTICKS, KNIVES, FORKS, AND SPOONS: While on the subject of bibs, I must say a word about eating. I was once told that the eaters of the world can be divided into three groups by the eating utensils, or lack of, they use. There are those who eat with their fingers, those who use chopsticks, and those who use knives, forks, and spoons. It is a cultural or even a class difference.

I remember as an adult, a year before my fiftieth birthday, sitting in stilted, grass hut in the Sulawesi, Indonesia. We were sitting with natives in a remote village about to share a feast. There were no dishes, no forks, and no chopsticks. Food was placed on palm leaves, and we dipped our fingers into the food in communal dishes.

At the time, I thought of my daughters when they were toddlers. They sat in high-chairs, with finger foods on the tray in front of them. Eating with their fingers seemed to be innate. It didn't have to be learned. As parents we began to teach them "civilized" ways, eating with forks and spoons.

People with disabilities and some older people have difficulty holding eating utensils or cutting food. There are all kinds of gadgets designed to help them. Rather than struggling to master them, why not be a kid again and use the innate tools we were born with—our fingers.

CLOTHING: If you have or had children, do you remember trying to dress them? It was a struggle for both parent and child. Putting on clothing is about the only thing I do not like about being a kid again.

Basically, I can dress myself. I use the word "basically" with a certain amount of fear and trepidation. When I first was diagnosed with ALS, people who had it longer told me stories about their experience of getting up in the morning. Their experience went something like this:

They get up in the morning pretty well rested. Then they would dress themselves. When they were finished dressing they were ready to go back to bed. So much for a good night's rest.

I hate buttons, have shoes with Velcro straps instead of laces, and cannot tie a tie. People need to put on my socks for me and in the winter help me putting on my down jacket. Putting on a winter jacket is one of the few amusing things about getting dressed.

Whenever a person struggles with me in putting on a jacket, it reminds me of putting snowsuits on my daughters when they were children. I thought that if I weren't careful I would break one of their arms while putting them in the sleeves. I have the suspicion that when they help me now they are thinking, "It's payback time."

So dressing is difficult, a struggle. The alternative is becoming a nudist. But, alas, not many in Minnesota go nude, especially in the winter months.

OH, TO SLEEP IN A CRIB AGAIN: The ALS Association of Minnesota has provided me with an adult crib. The more sophisticated would call it a hospital bed. Cribs are designed to keep children and babies from falling out of bed. My hospital bed does the same. The sides can be raised to keep me in.

Some child crib mattresses can be raised and lowered. My adult crib is much better. Not only does the mattress raise and lower, the head and feet can be raised and lowered separately.

My crib has a function for me that the makers probably never thought of when they designed it. Like many older people, with or without a chronic illness, I have difficulty dressing. I use the raising and lowering capacity for help in dressing. An example is putting on my pants. Sitting on the bed, I lower the mattress so I can slip my feet into the legs of the pants. Once that is done I raise the mattress so I can get into a standing position. As I raise the mattress I can pull my pants up around my waist so I can finish dressing. It's like having a new toy to help in my dressing.

Speaking of toys!

WHAT IS CHILDHOOD WITHOUT NEW TOYS?

I have many new toys since I moved to my new home in Minneapolis. I will mention only two of them.

I use to work out three times a week at a local spa in Connecticut. This happened through twelve years of having ALS. I was soon bothered by lack of muscle tone and flabbiness. Some of this was because of ALS. With the counsel of the physical and occupational therapist at the ALS clinic, I purchased a compact stationary cycle. It provides the same benefits as a cycle at the spa except you do not have climb onto it like a bicycle.

The compact cycle sits on the floor. I can sit in my wheelchair and peddle away. I can also put it on a table and use my arms and hands to peddle.

My second toy is much more interesting. As already mentioned, I have difficulty speaking. People I speak with, especially on the telephone, have difficulty understanding me.

The ALS Association and the Courage Center of Minnesota have provided me with an iPad. The iPad came with the Speak Up app. Programmed, it speaks for me. I use it primarily for phone conversations.

The unique thing about the program is that I can choose between a female or male voice and the type of accent I want. Since I am an Anglophile, my friends and Maxine, my speech therapist at the ALS clinic, thought I would pick the voice with an English accent. I did not.

I can preprogram certain phrases that are frequently used. To carry on a conversation, I type what I want to say on a touch keyboard, touch the speak button, and the iPad speaks for me.

The iPad also has all the buttons and whistles that other iPads have.

Some may say the compact cycle and the speaking iPad are marvels of technology. Returning to my childhood, I like to think of them as my new toys. Why not?

On the whole, childhood is a marvelous time of life. To be sure, it has its drawbacks. But a wonderful way to deal with a chronic illness or getting older is to accept and enjoy the many ways you are becoming a child again.

THE GIFT OF CAREGIVERS

When people are confronted with a chronic or life-threatening illness, there are usually one or two responses: the "why did it happen to me?" response and/or a period of depression. For some, with the passage of time, there is acceptance. We cope with the illness, seeing the limiting changes in our lives and manage to live with them as best we can. Others never accept their fate, and the depression never ends. This makes coping with the illness much more difficult.

Whatever our response, somehow we live with it. I deliberately left out the word "learning" because "living with it" is not something that we can be taught. Perhaps it is more of an instinct. This is not the case with our caregivers.

Our caregivers have a more difficult time than those of us with a chronic illness or disease. Not only do they see the person who has the chronic illness on a regular basis, often constantly, but they have to care for the basic needs of the individual. These needs can include bathing, dressing, and feeding. Sometimes they are loved ones who feel frustrated and helpless as they watch the disease or illness progress.

Once again, I am one of the fortunate ones. I continue to live alone, bathe, dress, prepare my own food, and feed myself. But I still need caregivers. I have a nurse who comes once a week, puts me through a range of motion exercises for my legs, and performs Healing Touch. She also takes me to the ALS Clinic, doctor, and dentist. I also have a person who cleans my home and does my laundry biweekly.

I am completely dependent on caregivers to get me out of the house. This is no easy task. It includes transferring me from my motorized wheelchair to a manually operated one and then requires that I am the pushed down the ramp that Bob Zimmerman designed. It also means collapsing the wheelchair so it will fit into the trunk of the car. When we arrive at our destination the reverse process is required. Since the process takes a lot of energy and time, I put off many needed errands. I am reminded of this each time I go for a haircut. My hair is longer than it used to be in the seventies. I am tempted to make my massive hair on the back of my neck into a ponytail.

Not everyone can perform the task of getting me out of the house. One of my closest friends used to take me out to many places but now due to her own physical limits, she is no longer able to do so.

In the winter there is the added chore of helping me into my winter jacket and dealing with inclement weather. Pushing a wheelchair through snow is not easy.

Many care organizations, like the ALS Association, realize the crucial role caregivers play in the case of chronically ill and the elderly. They provide respite times for caregivers. It could be a full day for themselves or a night on the town with friends.

Caregivers are the unsung heroes for those of us with chronic illness. They suffer along with us. I am told that their caring often affects them. Caregivers need to be celebrated and cared for. They are a unique gift. Seeing the ups and downs of the person they are caring for, the changes, and the deterioration, caregivers remain focused on providing comfort and the care needed. Indeed, they are a gift.

CAREGIVERS COME IN ALL SHAPES, SIZES, AND AGES: Originally, this chapter on caregivers ended with the above paragraph. That all changed on December 22, 2013, when an unexpected caregiver entered my life.

My daughter and I attended *The Nutcracker* performed by Ballet Minnesota. A friend of my daughter danced the role of the whimsical Uncle Drosselmeyer. It is a role he has played and danced for over fifteen years.

While this performance of *The Nutcracker* was one of the best I have seen, the audience and where I was seated were just as inspirational as what happened on stage. It was a matinee performance and children outnumbered the adults. I was sitting in the section reserved for wheelchairs. The boy seated on my left was held in his wheelchair by a strap and unable to talk. It was difficult to judge his age, but my guess is that he was about five. His mother sat next to him in a regular theater seat.

During the first act, the boy would take his hand and brush my arm. It wasn't until the second act that I realized that the boy wanted me to hold his hand. His mother held and rubbed one hand and I the other. The boy was animated by the performance. With effort he clapped when the audience clapped. Like the eighty-one-year-old man sitting next to him, no sound was made by their clapping hands.

When the performance was over, his mother, father, and grandmother thanked me for being so kind to the boy. I said, "No. I should thank you and thank you for being such good parents."

Two people in wheelchairs—one an old man and the other a young boy—sitting next to each other. Neither could talk nor adequately care for himself. Yet we were of a kindred spirit—offering care to one another. For a brief moment in time we were bound together hearing music that was composed by a Russian over one hundred years ago—nurturing each other.

I think of a verse in the Hebrew Bible that ends with the words "a little child shall lead them."

My little companion made the true miracle of this season a reality in my life. Two lives holding hands and nurturing each other.

Most of this section was included in my annual holiday greeting, including the quotation from the Hebrew Bible, Isaiah 1:16. I have now learned the name of my caregiver, the little boy in the wheelchair. His name? Isaiah.

THE GIFT OF MOTOR NEURONS' INNER RESOURCES

I was asked to give a presentation to my ALS support group on how faith can help with ALS. I decided to talk about "Motor Neurons' Inner Resources." I only talked about faith and/or religion when they helped to tap into, or reinforce, our inner resources—resources that all of us are born with. Most Western religions do not always equip us to use these inner resources on a regular basis or to use them when catastrophes occur in our lives. Perhaps "spirituality" is a better term than "faith." Following is what I shared with the group.

The temperature was well below zero outside a town in northern Wisconsin called Shawno. I was in an Alexian abbey that was occupied on January 1, 1975, by a group of Menomonee Indians called the Warrior Society. I was there as a negotiator for the governor of Wisconsin, Patrick Lucey.

Many members of the Warrior Society brought their families with them into the abbey, and a number of them had the flu. Some of them had high fevers. The Indians sent for a medicine man from South Dakota.

I spent time talking to the medicine man, who was dressed in a buckskin jacket with a bag of healing herbs hanging around his neck. It was the first time I had met a medicine man, and I was curious about his background. He explained that the title and healing powers were passed down through his family line. He also shared that he was a member of the AMA and had received his medical degree from the University of Minnesota.

We talked into the night about his belief in his scientific training as a doctor and his belief in the traditional healing powers of a medicine man. My new found friend saw little difference between the two. He viewed both as a part of the nature that each person is born with.

I told my support group that I was one of the fortunate ones with ALS. My symptoms, primarily in my upper motor neuron system as previously mentioned, are progressing slowly. When I was finally diagnosed, my world fell apart. When the initial shock had passed, I began to read everything I could about ALS. I read every book and article on the brain I could get my hands on.

One day I saw a new book about the brain called *Why God Won't Go Away*. It was written by two scientists, Andrew Newberg and Eugene d'Aquili. Dr. Newberg, an MD, teaches in the Department of Radiology and Nuclear Medicine at the University of Pennsylvania and had at that time spent six years studying the brain and its functions. Eugene d'Aquili is also an MD and a PhD. He teaches in the Department of Psychiatry at the same university.

These two men found that by attaching electrodes to the brain (EEG) while a person was meditating, or centering as the Quakers call it, a particular bundle of neurons was stimulated, which they call the association area. They found that that same portion of the brain was stimulated by any religious or meditative experience like yoga, prayer—experiences that help us escape, if you will, from ordinary day-to-day experiences.

They also found that when that portion of the brain was stimulated, it drew from or was integrated with all other portions of the brain. They concluded from this that all centers of the brain feed into that bundle of neurons that compels the "spiritual urge." Religious experience, they surmised, has its roots in biology.

I don't know whether Newberg and d'Aquili are right in their conclusions, but they and our medicine man confirmed what I have always believed, that we too often separate our lives into mind and body or mind and spirit. This is certainly true of those of us born into Western cultures. We have even westernized our religions. Both Judaism and Christianity are, whether we admit it or not, Eastern religions. Most of us have lost the ability of linking or seeing the relationship of mind, body, and spirit. We westernized the coping, healing, and yes, the escaping powers that make us whole and help handle day-to-day problems or diseases like ALS.

I would like to expand the concepts of faith, religion, and spirituality. These enlargements certainly include what we traditionally have thought of as prayer or the reading of Hebrew, Christian, and Muslim scriptures. But even when we do these, we often go about it the wrong way. We pray but we don't listen. We read but we don't think. Broadening these traditional methods taps us into our inner self—the motor neurons that Newberg and d'Aquili found connect us to that "spiritual urge." Whether we are religious or not, these are available to all of us for they are a part our very nature.

As I have already written, shortly after I was diagnosed with ALS I was walking briskly to do an errand. Realizing that there was a possibility I would not be able to do this in the future, I slowed my pace and started to take in what I normally would miss. I stopped to smell the flowers. I walked at a snail's pace, and like a snail, I savored every moment.

I. The first in enlarging our concept of spirituality: the SMELL THE FLOWERS APPROACH. Savor the ordinary things in life. When we are faced with what we are told is on a collision course with death, we can do that. Whether it is a grandchild laughing, enjoying each bite of food, or, God forbid, that wonderful chocolate- or latte-flavored Ensure. By doing this as a kid again, we will tap into that "spiritual urge" of those other motor neurons and receive comfort and strength.

II. The second is called TAPPING RESOURCES WITH A NEW VISION. It may be scriptures, inspirational reading, poetry, fiction, music, or watching a movie. It can be deep. It can be light. By "a new vision" I mean using the right side of the brain. When I received my first issue of *The Light*, a publication of the Connecticut ALS Association, I read some of the poems and inspirational readings selected by Joan Argento, the patient service coordinator. My initial reaction was something like "isn't that nice." When I picked them up again I let them speak to me. They were no longer mere words on paper. I absorbed them. They inspired and lightened my load.

Our tastes are different. Tapping into life with a new vision for me is learning from the Eastern and Native American cultures. It is reading a poem by Maya Angelou, attending a musical, watching Wisconsin football, or immersing myself in world affairs.

I told the group that we who have ALS and our caregivers already tap into resources, or everyday tasks, with a new vision. I am not sure we would say with Lou Gehrig that "I am the luckiest man on the face of the earth." When you have a chronic disease that may be terminal, you look at things and events in a different light. Every day events take on new meaning. Perhaps we have already tapped into that "spiritual" bundle of neurons. We need to cultivate and strengthen the new vision we have and help others to discover it.

III. The third area in expanding the concepts of faith, religion, and spirituality is the most difficult, perhaps because it is most foreign to us and our culture. It is less foreign to Roman Catholics than Protestants. Orthodox Jews understand it more than Reform Jews. I call this the RELAX AND RETREAT MODE OF FAITH AND SPIRITUALITY.

We Americans are always on the go. As a friend of mine said, "We even work at our play." The relax and retreat mode involves many forms. To some it is meditation, while to others it is yoga. Native Americans have a communal sweat lodge and their vision quest. Whether alone or with others, it is a time to be alone with your thoughts and center down on what is most important to you. It may involve prayer. It is much more about listening than talking.

It has taken me a lifetime to learn how to relax and retreat. For me it is best to be alone with a good CD playing and sitting in candlelight. I put all thoughts out of my mind. At times I may be reading a book when some thought grabs me. I concentrate on that thought, and a whole series of ideas and thoughts enter my mind. The end result is a feeling of relaxation and a clearer idea of who I am, how I can face obstacles, and my place in the world.

All these concepts may seem strange to some because they are new. I find they work for me. They help me to find my center and tap into resources that are a part of our nature as human beings.

I concluded my talk to my support group by going back to our medicine man and the two scientists. All three linked science and faith or spirituality. In fact, the authors write that the concept of God exists in a bundle of neurons in our brain. Whether you believe in God or not, the essence of inner resources for healing, coping, and doing are a part of every human being. I truly believe this.

It seems to me that those of us who have ALS have a head start on most people. Our disease centers in the motor neuron system. Newberg and d'Aquili have found that the association area that compels the "spiritual urge" is located in the same system. Our brains are not that large. Our ALS and "the God who won't go away" can't be that far apart. All we have to do is link them up by:

SMELLING THE FLOWERS
TAPPING RESOURCES WITH A NEW VISION
RELAXING AND RETREATING

THE GIFT OF RACING WITH HORSES

ORIGINALITY

I preface this chapter with a word of caution to myself. Very few people have original thoughts, ideas, or philosophies. Rather, we build upon the ideas, thoughts, and philosophies of others until they become our own. Over the course of time the original source becomes lost. People often claim themselves as the originator, when they are not. I make no such claim here.

Frankly, the original source has been lost. How it is applied to ALS or any other illness or any crisis in life is my own.

Dr. David McLennan, who for many years was minister of Brick Presbyterian Church in Rochester, New York, may have been the original source. He was one of my preaching professors at Colgate Rochester Divinity

School in the same city. McLennan was a popular, riveting preacher. He was a scholar and spoke the common language of the people.

THE BIBLICAL PREMISE

There is a wonderful story in the Hebrew Bible. The prophet Jeremiah, much like Job, complains to God. He did everything that God told him to do to bring his people back to righteousness and the way of God. The people did not change. They continued in their "wicked" ways.

Jeremiah complained, "...you are near in their mouth and far from their heart..."

This was Jeremiah's way of saying, "The people talk the talk but do not walk the walk."

Too often in our complaints or talks with God, we do all the talking and never listen for a response. Fortunately, Jeremiah receives a response. Perhaps it was not the response that Jeremiah expected.

"If you have raced with men on foot and they have wearied you, how will you compete with horses?"

This was God's way of saying to Jeremiah, "You think you have problems now? Just wait until the situations you face get out of control and are insurmountable."

How Jeremiah faced future difficulties was entirely up to him. We humans have the freedom of choice in approaching any problems or difficulties in life. How do we apply it to problems related to our physical life? I will draw from my experience with ALS, but it can be applied to any illness, disease, or problem in life.

When we approach any problems in life we have three choices:

- We can run away from the problem.
- We can run against the problem.
- We can run with the problem and seize life, *carpe diem.*

I have seen all three approaches from people with ALS. In fact, they reflect, in part, my own experience with the illness.

RUNNING AWAY FROM THE PROBLEM

Running away from ALS, any health crisis, or problems in life takes many forms.

Many people take this denial approach. I really don't have the disease. The doctor could be wrong. We take the attitude that "I will be the exception to the rule."

Some people become recluses. I am in and out of this mode. A person takes this approach because he or she thinks that people will think they are odd because of (strange) speech patterns and difficulties with eating, walking, or strength. This just exacerbates the already existing problem.

RUNNING AGAINST THE PROBLEM

Still other people treat any life-threatening illness as though they were running a race, a competition against the disease or illness. I am reminded of the song from the musical *The Pajama Game*:

"Hurry up, hurry up, hurry up, hurry up
can't waste time
when you're racing with the clock"

However, it is true with ALS, or any disease, that we are racing for a cure. We do everything, including raising money to fund research and increasing public awareness, to find a cure.

I find it futile to race against my ALS. I literally am wasting time when I should be concentrating with all my caregivers on making life productive, enjoyable, and comfortable.

RUNNING WITH THE PROBLEM

The best way of handling ALS or any problem we face is to control (run) the problem and not let the problem control us. I have found that the best way to take control is to use the example of others.

An excellent example for me was Clarissa. She was a newcomer to my ALS support group in Connecticut. She was a vivacious young woman in her twenties. People in the support group were captivated by her outgoing spirit, her frankness, and her positive attitude.

Clarissa seemed comfortable in her wheelchair as though she had sat in it for many years. She had. She had been born with Spina bifida and lived with it for over twenty years. To add to her problems, she was diagnosed with ALS at the age of twenty-one.

Despite Clarissa's health problems, her positive spirit was contagious. At each support group, her presence gave a boost to everyone. Clarissa died from ALS at the age of twenty-three.

Clarissa chose not to let ALS and Spina bifida take charge of her life. She chose to run with both of those dreaded diseases. Clarissa knew how to run with horses.

When each of the support group members had contact with Clarissa, she gave us hope to fight on. I think of her every day. Those of us who were touched by her presence marveled at her positive spirit and were undergirded by it to try to face our own future with ALS in the same spirit.

Clarissa squarely faced both her Spina bifida and ALS every day of her life. Neither dampened her spirit. She ran her diseases. By doing so, she savored each moment of every day.

FINAL REFLECTIONS ON ALS, MY GIFT

Before I had ALS, I marveled at the changes taking place in our world. I still do. Like Juan Ponce de Leon, I wanted to discover that "Fountain of Youth" so I wouldn't miss any of the amazing world taking shape around me. With ALS, I thought that my world was shattered. After the initial shock wave swept through my whole being, I realized that this was just one of the changes taking place in my personal world.

My ALS soon became a new adventure for me. If my ALS runs its normal course there may come a time when I will lose the capacity to speak entirely and lose the ability to use my limbs. And unless some miracle discovery is found, my ALS may follow its normal course and I will eventually die from it. Do I feel sorry for myself? No. A WHOLE NEW WORLD is waiting to be discovered.

I am continuously reminded of a poem written by the Scottish poet Charlotte (Lottie) Sinclair. Her poems are not too well known because some of them were only published in the local press in Aberdeen, Scotland. The poem is "I'm Fine Thank You." It is about growing old but can apply to many conditions in life. As one who is a "young" eighty-one years old and has the "designer disease," ALS, Sinclair's poem expresses some of my own reflections.

There is nothing the matter with me
I'm as healthy as can be.
I have arthritis in both my knees
And when I talk, I talk with a wheeze,
My pulse is weak and my blood is thin,
But I'm awfully well for the shape I'm in.

The moral is this—as my tale I unfold,
That for you and me who are growing old,
It's better to say, "I'm fine" with a grin,
Than to let folks know the shape we're in.

This portion of doggerel poetry taps into the humor of living with ALS. Charlotte Sinclair died in 2010 at the age of ninety-seven.

Ms. Pavia, my first speech therapist, shared a newspaper article with me. The headline read, "Learning

How to Die." It is about retired US Air Force Major Michael Donnelly of Vernon, Connecticut. Donnelly served in the Gulf War and has ALS. The article is written by Don Pesci of Manchester, Connecticut, where I lived.

Pesci begins his article with a quotation from Michel de Montaigne: "To philosophize is to learn how to die." It is not the quote that I would have chosen. A much better quote would have been "Mon métieretmon art, c'est vivre" (To know how to live is all my calling and all my art).

I have been philosophizing a great deal since I was diagnosed with ALS. To me, to philosophize is to know how to live. Like Horace, I have *carpe diem*, seized the day. The full quote from Horace should be noted: "Time will have been running. Snatch the sleeve of today, and trust as little as you may to tomorrow."

I would do anything not to have ALS. But I have it. I can feel sorry for myself, but I don't. For some reason the disease has given me a clearer view and appreciation for life and the whole new world around me. Like Horace, I am snatching the sleeve of today, but unlike him, I trust in tomorrow.

THE GIFT OF LESSONS TAUGHT

- ❖ Do not believe your doctor. This is a blunt way of saying, "Get a second opinion." In my case, I had the opinions of two internists and three neurologists and the work of many specialists before I was diagnosed.
- ❖ Read voraciously about your illness, but do not believe everything you read. I read everything I could get my hands on about ALS and scoured the Internet. I am still reading and still learning.
- ❖ Statistics are averages. The average life expectancy after diagnosis for ALS is from two to five years. But the progress and how it develops is different for everyone. Like many diseases, ALS is a "designer disease." It is different for everyone. Life can stretch out for twenty years or more.

- Whether you have a life-threatening disease or not—GET YOUR HOUSE IN ORDER. When there was a hint that something was wrong with me, I drafted a living will, a durable power of attorney, and a will. I had put this off for sixty years because I was healthy.
- Get acquainted with a teaching or research hospital and know its resources as well as its limitations. The same is true with organizations created to find and fund research to help people with a particular disease. The ALS Association and the Muscular Dystrophy Association (MDA) have been a constant help and resource to me.
- Shore up your support groups. You may not be aware of them, but they are many. They could be family and friends, a plethora of caregivers, or support groups made up of people who share your disease or malady.
- Anticipate and plan for changes that will take place in your life.
- Beware of quack theories, but explore alternative methods of dealing with the limitations, physical problems, and emotional problems that come with the disease.
- Live life to the fullest.
- Keep a sense of humor, and don't play on people's sympathies.

- ❖ Never give up hope. New medical discoveries are happening every day. One day it will be our turn.
- ❖ Always remember that every new experience is a gift, no matter how negative or devastating it may be. I did. My life is both rich and full, a gift of the "designer disease," ALS.

ABOUT THE AUTHOR

Willis (Bill) Merriman was diagnosed with ALS twenty years ago upon retirement. In his retirement he moved to Connecticut to ski, travel, and write. Although he has spent a considerable amount of his time writing about his many eclectic interests, much of Bill's writing has been about his journey with ALS. This booklet is about that journey.

An ordained minister of the United Church Christ, Bill spent most of his career working with ecumenical and interfaith agencies throughout the country and around the world. His work and his life have been devoted to helping those less fortunate—being their advocate and at times their voice. Now his voice is *his* voice—as someone living with ALS. Bill's voice can also serve as the voice for anyone suffering a debilitating disease. His thoughtful, reflective wisdom and optimism provide messages of hope and of the benefits of maintaining a positive attitude.

Made in the USA
San Bernardino, CA
24 April 2016